MW01592324

TABLE OF CONTENTS

HOW TO USE THIS JOURNAL

If you've purchased the accompanying Little Book of Self-Love, you'll see that the layout of this journal loosely follows the book. This is so you can use them together to enhance your journey. This goes for the Little Box of Self-Love as well. All three products are designed to work together to deepen your self-discovery while you make your way through this experience.

You don't need the book or the box to use this journal successfully, however, it is the most impactful and enjoyable when all three are used simultaneously.

You can choose your own pace and method in any way that serves you best. With that said, because it's set up to follow the layout of the Little Book of Self-Love, you will find that starting at the beginning of this journal and working your way through in a linear fashion will make more sense. This is because the lessons build as the journal progresses.

The design is meant to be simple, led with thought-provoking prompts and a few exercises to challenge what you think you know about yourself. The goal is to identify the self-limiting beliefs getting in your way of living the life you've always wanted and deserve.

If you'd like to learn more about the Little Book of Self-Love and/or the Little Box of Self-Love, please go to elizabeth-craig.com/shop.

Disclaimer and important note to readers

This journal has been written and published for informational purposes only. The author is not a healthcare provider. This journal is not intended to serve as medical or mental health advice or to serve as any form of treatment.

INTRODUCTION

she woke up
every morning
with the option of
being anyone she wished

how beautiful it was
that she always chose
herself.

—tyler kent white

This poem is the Holy Grail of intentions I set with this journal. This book is meant to lead you through a journey into the self in a way that challenges what you think you know about yourself; it's meant to be a reckoning of sorts. If you accept this invitation, the mission is to become whole again. You will collect every misplaced puzzle piece and graciously, lovingly, and forgivingly place them right back where they belong. You will do this with a newfound wisdom and clarity you never knew you had because you will have taken the time to learn about and build the most precious relationship you could ever have. You guessed it; your relationship with yourself.

You have everything you have ever needed inside of you to take this step, and you always have, friend

ONE

Your Journey

This section is best completed after reading the chapter 'A Journey Gone Awry' in the
Little Book of Self-Love

rather than believing
you are trying to find
something,
consider that your
quest is a
rediscovering of that
which you never
truly lost.

-present-

What occurrences, thoughts, behaviors, or patterns have you experienced that have encouraged you to begin or delve deeper into your self-love journey?

Would you consider any of these experiences to be negative? Positive? How so?

If you listed any positive experiences, discuss how they made you feel or what shifts they made in your life.

_____

_____

_____

_____

_____

_____

_____

_____

_____

_____

_____

_____

_____

_____

_____

_____

If you listed any negative experiences, discuss how they made you feel or impacted your feelings about yourself.

TAKE YOUR POWER BACK

Blaming others or certain experiences for your circumstances in life gives the person or event your power. Only you have the authority to decide how any act or occurrence will affect you.

Regarding the previous question, do you believe it's possible to reframe your thoughts and reclaim your power?

EXERCISE:

- Write the story of a sensitive or uncomfortable event from your life that you believe affected your feelings of self-love.
- Rather than viewing yourself as the Victim in this story, take a moment to consider how you might be a Creator instead. Rather than viewing the other person or event as the Perpetrator, consider how they might be a Challenger instead.
- What can you positively *create* from the pain of this event? How has this person or event *challenged* you to grow and evolve into a better version of yourself? Write three ideas for each of these two questions.
- How might you use the answers from the question above in your daily life to heal and move forward?

_____

_____

_____

_____

_____

_____

_____

_____

_____

_____

TWO

What is Self-Love?

This section is best completed after reading the chapter 'What is Self-Love?' in the
Little Book of Self-Love

SELF-LOVE

Believing you deserve to love and be loved simply because you exist. Trusting in the divine right to believe in and love yourself, and seek and experience happiness, regardless of what others believe about you. It transcends physical beauty and is in alignment with your most authentic self.

What is your definition of self-love?

_____

_____

_____

_____

_____

_____

_____

_____

_____

_____

_____

_____

_____

_____

_____

_____

_____

Who in your life do you believe supports your journey of self-love? How do you think they help you in a loving, nurturing, and encouraging way?

_____

_____

_____

_____

_____

_____

_____

_____

_____

_____

_____

_____

_____

_____

_____

_____

_____

Is there anyone in your life blocking your journey? In what ways do you think this is occurring and what do you think you can do to find balance?

_____

_____

_____

_____

_____

_____

_____

_____

_____

_____

_____

_____

_____

_____

_____

_____

_____

What personal boundaries would help shield you from unsupportive people while giving you the space and time to engage in activities to further your journey?

What things do you love most about yourself?

What are your best qualities?

_____

_____

_____

_____

_____

_____

_____

_____

_____

_____

_____

_____

_____

_____

_____

_____

_____

_____

Is it difficult to believe positive things people say about you? If so, why?

_____

_____

_____

_____

_____

_____

_____

_____

_____

_____

_____

_____

_____

_____

_____

_____

_____

_____

Let's shift your perspective.

EXERCISE:

- Write a personal eulogy for yourself and make sure to include:

    - Everything you're proud of
    - What and whom you will miss the most
    - What you believe people will miss most about you

You might think this is a weird exercise, but hear me out. You may be surprised at how cathartic it can be to write about your life in this way because it helps to see yourself from an entirely different perspective than you're used to.

_____

_____

_____

_____

_____

_____

_____

_____

_____

_____

Did anything surprise you about what you wrote? If so, what?

_____

_____

_____

_____

_____

_____

_____

_____

_____

_____

_____

_____

_____

_____

_____

_____

_____

Let's shift your perspective a little further.

EXERCISE:

- Ask someone close to you to write a eulogy about you and include:

    - Everything about you for which they are proud
    - What they believe you will miss the most
    - What they will miss most about you

Feel free to cut out and paste it in this section, or rewrite it.

_____

_____

_____

_____

_____

_____

_____

_____

_____

_____

_____

_____

_____

Did anything surprise you about what your loved one wrote? If so, what?

If you could see yourself the way that others do, you'd wish you were as beautiful as you.

--Jon Bon Jovi

THREE

Building a Relationship with Yourself

This section is best completed after reading the chapters 'Myths of Self-Love', 'Taking Action', and 'Tidbits to Keep in Mind' in the Little Book of Self-Love

Suffering is universal. Victimhood is optional.

--Dr. Edith Eger

What do you need more or less of in your life to help you feel more connected to yourself? Some examples may include creativity, exercise, or curiosity. What can you implement in your life to work towards a deeper inner connection?

If money or time was no object and you couldn't fail, what would you try?

What can you do to give yourself more time for self-care?

_____

_____

_____

_____

_____

_____

_____

_____

_____

_____

_____

_____

_____

_____

_____

Do you often neglect self-care to take care of others? When and why?

Do you believe your needs are less of a priority than others? If so, how?

_____

_____

_____

_____

_____

_____

_____

_____

_____

_____

_____

_____

_____

_____

_____

_____

_____

Consider a recent occasion when you put someone's care ahead of your own. Rewrite the story as you would have preferred it to have occurred.

What does your ideal day look like?

What does your ideal life look like?

_____

_____

_____

_____

_____

_____

_____

_____

_____

_____

_____

_____

_____

_____

_____

_____

_____

_____

If you could live your ideal life in any way you desired, knowing it wouldn't hurt anyone or take away from any of your loved ones in any manner, would your answer to the previous question change and, if so, how?

If you answered yes to the previous question, is there any part of your new answer that you could incorporate into your current life to work towards your ideal life? If so, what?

_____

_____

_____

_____

_____

_____

_____

_____

_____

_____

_____

_____

_____

_____

_____

_____

What actions can you take in your life that will bring you closer to your ideal life?

EXERCISE:

- Describe three actions in which you are currently engaging to work towards your ideal life. (You may think the answer is nothing, but did deep; I guarantee you are doing at least three things that are moving you in a forward direction. They don't have to be big actions.)
- Describe three actions you can take in your current life that will bring you closer to your ideal life. Examples may include reading certain books, attending certain workshops, traveling, relocating, or searching for a new job.
- What three actions can you describe that you may not be able to fulfill right now but could set as future goals?

_____

_____

_____

_____

_____

_____

_____

_____

_____

Let nothing
come between
you and you.

- relationship goals -

FOUR

Living Authentically

This section is best completed after reading the chapter 'The Big Secret' in the Little Book of Self-Love

*Being vulnerable
doesn't mean
you're weak;
it means
you're brave.*

- don't pretend -

Do you find it difficult to be vulnerable? Are you uncomfortable expressing emotions in front of loved ones? If so, why?

_____

_____

_____

_____

_____

_____

_____

_____

_____

_____

_____

_____

_____

_____

_____

_____

How do you think being vulnerable could shift your relationships, and perhaps your capacity for true joy? What can you do to encourage more vulnerability in your life?

When are you saying 'yes' when you want to say 'no'? When are you saying 'no' when you want to say 'yes'?

Who do you believe benefits the most when you say 'yes' when you want to say 'no', or 'no' when you want to say 'yes'? How and why?

What changes can you make that might help you confidently speak your needs and your truth more openly?

_____

_____

_____

_____

_____

_____

_____

_____

_____

_____

_____

_____

_____

_____

_____

_____

_____

What do you believe you need to let go of to move forward in your life?

_____

_____

_____

_____

_____

_____

_____

_____

_____

_____

_____

_____

_____

_____

_____

_____

_____

_____

How can you practice more self-compassion and self-forgiveness?

_____

_____

_____

_____

_____

_____

_____

_____

_____

_____

_____

_____

_____

_____

_____

_____

_____

Do you believe your friends, siblings, children, family members, and other loved ones in your life deserve to live freely, seek joy, and prioritize their contentment and care as equally as everyone else's in their life? If not, why? If so, why?

Do you believe everyone deserves to live a joyful and satisfying life?

EXERCISE:

- What advice would you give to a friend who appears exhausted because she can't seem to get her family to help her with any of the daily tasks in their home?
- What advice would you give to a friend who continuously talks about things she would do for herself if she could only find the time?
- What advice would you give to a friend whose family member or friend appears to impose things upon her at her own expense, resulting in her neglecting her care and happiness?
- What advice would you give a friend you suspect believes she's unworthy of engaging in activities that make her happy and satisfied?

_____

_____

_____

_____

_____

_____

_____

_____

_____

_____

Considering your answers to the previous exercise, do you believe you deserve to live freely, seek joy, and prioritize your contentment and care as equally as everyone else's in your life? If not, why? If so, why?

If you answered yes to the question above, do you think you are living in alignment with this belief? If so, how? If not, why?

Being clear is kind. Being unclear is unkind.

--Brené Brown

RITUALS

It took a long time for me to understand the benefits of rituals. I know that word makes it sound like I'm in a black robe walking slowly through a forest at midnight while chanting in a different language, but I hate to disappoint you. I mean, yeah...OK, I'm sure there are some interesting and unique practices out there. But for this journal, I'm simply talking about putting a succession of actions together that activate your senses, emotions, and energy, all to promote self-love.

Simplicity is key here.

What I love about rituals is that they are an active way for me to release anything I want to release. I can reset any part of myself that needs a moment of stillness, infuse myself with power and intention, and simply honor, celebrate, and show my appreciation for all of the blessings that have been granted to me.

As with everything you incorporate into your life in any way, make sure any ritual in which you choose to participate works for you and makes you feel good. You should always walk away from any ritual feeling refreshed and rejuvenated. If you don't, you may want to spend some time considering whether you were simply releasing something or perhaps that the ritual you activated wasn't for you.

There are quite a lot of different rituals you can practice but you can also make up any kind you want or modify any existing ritual to fit your desires. There are no rules, and there are no specific ingredients. The point is to engage while incorporating actions that have a distinct meaning for you.

I am including my favorite rituals in this section and they have either been made up by me or are pieces of others I found while researching, and then adapted to my liking. If you like what you see here, use them to your heart's content, but also feel free to modify them in any way that feels good to you.

If you're interested in taking a deeper dive into your self-love journey, make sure to pick the Little Book of Self-Love, if you haven't already. If you've purchased the accompanying Little Box of Self-Love, you can use what has been included in the rituals below. If not, feel free to use whatever you have.

Before we dive into rituals, you'll see I've included the following section on clearing, grounding, replenishing, and shielding. This is a wonderful practice that I incorporate into my life as often as I can, and also before I start any rituals, meditations, tarot sessions, or any activity that requires my full presence in body, mind, and soul. It's a simple way to set your energy up for success.

CLEARING. GROUNDING. REPLENISHING. SHIELDING.

CLEARING

I start with clearing because it rids my energetic body of any stagnancy that needs to be released and gets it ready to accept some good energy to replace it. This will clear any old, leftover, or unused energy that no longer serves you and any energy you've picked up from others. Clearing dumps all of this unusable energy that has attached to you along the way and has bogged you down. It is so refreshing to clear!

Clearing can be as simple as taking deep belly breaths and imagining that you're collecting all of that energy up that needs to be cleared on each inhale, and either breathing it out and imagining it returning to the Earth or releasing it down your legs and through your feet.

Tip: make sure to ask Mother Earth if you have permission to dump this energy back into the Earth before you begin. You will typically feel an instant "yes", and remember to say "thank you".

You can also achieve clearing by using a smudge stick, such as Palo Santo, or dried Rosemary, Lavender, or Yerba Santa. There are a lot of varieties when it comes to smudge sticks. You will see this method being used in the Rituals section of this book. To clear with a smudge stick, light your stick of choice and blow out the flame to allow it to smoke. Wave the stick and smoke from the top of your body to the bottom, both front and back. As you do this, ask the smoke to clear any energy that no longer serves you so that space can be made for energy that does. This manner of clearing can also be used to clear any physical space as well.

A little note regarding smudging. As you engage in practices like smudging, it's crucial to respect the cultural significance behind them. While many embrace this ritual for its cleansing properties, it's equally important to honor its origins and traditions. In this spirit, you are encouraged to refrain from using culturally significant ingredients unless you are part of the respective indigenous communities. Let's cultivate mindfulness and respect in our spiritual practices, honoring the wisdom and traditions of those who have entrusted us with these sacred rituals.

My favorite way to clear is called the Ring of Fire, which was taught to me by my Reiki Master. I've modified it a little to suit my needs and you can feel free to do the same.

How to Clear

- Imagine that you have a big bonfire above your head, and it transforms into a huge ring of fire that is big enough to fit over your body. Now, imagine that another fire ring appears in a mirror image below the initial ring.

- Visualize the double ring of fire moving slowly down your body from your crown to your feet while burning off the energy that no longer serves you as it moves. If you understand what
- chakras are and where your seven main chakras are located in your body, imagine each time the ring of fire glides over each of

them, it is clearing that chakra as well. Make sure to visualize the ring of fire clearing the front *and* the back of the body.

- Once the ring reaches your feet, imagine the ring becoming a lit paper lantern and then ask Mother Earth if you can send it down into the earth to be recycled. When you feel a "yes", imagine the lit paper lantern, with all of the energy you've cleared, floating down into the earth and disappearing.

- If you don't have enough time for this on a particular day, you can also use a Selenite wand (like the one included in the Little Box of Self-Love). Glide it down the front, sides, and back of the body about four inches away. Selenite is a cleansing and clearing stone and a wonderful way to clear stuck or stagnant energy in a pinch.

You are now clear!

GROUNDING

Now that you have an empty vessel, you can connect to Mother Earth and not only ground but also fill yourself back up with Her nurturing energy. The Earth is electrically charged and humans are bioelectric beings. We are meant to be connected to the Earth, which provides strength, stability, and balance. When we take time to connect into this energy, we are less stressed, and anxious, and are much more centered and solid.

Grounding is simple and easy to do. To ground, take your shoes off and sit or walk barefoot in the grass for 5 or 10 minutes. This is also known as earthing. Anytime you are touching the earth, you are grounding. Does this sound too woo-woo? Look it up. It's a real, bonafide, scientific method and it works. Seasoned travelers know this trick. It's a great way to combat and eliminate jet lag.

If you can't touch the earth for some reason, here is a simple mental practice that I use.

How to Ground

- Sit on the floor or in a chair with your back straight and feet firmly planted on the floor.

- Close your eyes and get your breathing into a slow rhythm. Inhale for three counts, filling the belly first, and then the lungs with each breath, then slowly breathe out for four counts.

- Once you are in this rhythm (approximately three breaths), continue breathing in three counts, then begin to imagine roots growing out of the bottoms of your feet and into the Earth. Imagine thick roots growing through the floor, then the foundation of the building you're in, traveling into the soil and continuing into each layer of the Earth until you reach the center.

- Next, imagine that little rootlets are growing out of each thick root and multiplying so much you can feel that deep connection with the Earth. Sit in this for as long as you like.

- Imagine that you are trying to lift each foot. If you can "lift" either easily (mentally, not literally), imagine those rootlets grabbing on tighter until you imagine your feet are so rooted you can't lift them.

Now you're grounded.

REPLENISHING

Now that you are grounded, what you previously emptied can be refilled. Not replenishing your energetic body leaves you open to being filled right back up with energy just like you got rid of. Replenishing keeps you fueled and strong for the day. The two ways I like to do this is with the energy of Mother Earth first, then from Spirit. You don't have to do both if you don't feel it and one will certainly do. The choice is yours.

How to Replenish

- Ask Mother Earth if you can fill yourself with her energy. Close your eyes and imagine a gold, brilliant light filling each rootlet and traveling up through your body, up to your crown.

- Ask Spirit the same question. Imagine white light filling your entire body, starting at the top of the head.

- Imagine your crown chakra opening, or if you're unfamiliar with chakras, imagine white light coming into your body from the top of your head.

- Visualize the light filling every space of your body from head to toe, in both the front and the back of your body.

You have now filled yourself with the nurturing, loving, and healing energies from Spirit and Mother Earth.

NOTES

SELF-LOVE RITUAL

This ritual is for when you need a reminder of why you're worth loving (and you are). Taking the time to acknowledge and honor yourself is the epitome of self-love. It's the act of saying Me Before You, and if that sounds a bit self-centered, remember this saying from earlier in the book: self-love is not self-ish. When you focus on inner love, you're filling yourself up with all you'll need to give to others. I can't impress upon you how important this is.

What You'll Need

- A mirror (a large one you can sit in front of is best, but any mirror will do)

- Journal/pen

- Smudge stick for clearing your space

- Incense and incense holder, or a diffuser with bergamot, rose, juniper, ylang ylang, frankincense, or lavender essential oil. You can also spray the Moonwater from the Little Box of Self-Love, if available.

- Smokey Quartz, Rose Quartz, and Amethyst crystals

- Love Notes (from the box. Optional)

Ritual Steps

1. Find a comfortable and quiet space where you won't be disturbed and smudge the space for clearing.
2. Light the incense or diffuser and as the smoke/steam billows, concentrate on what you are asking for in this ritual and what you want for the outcome.
3. If using, find a place to set your Love Notes near you. Before setting them down, read them and let the messages integrate.
4. Set your mirror in front of you so that you can see as much of yourself as possible.
5. While holding one of your crystals in your left hand (receiving side of the body), focus on yourself in the mirror and allow any thoughts to arise.
6. As your thoughts arise, notice if they are positive or negative. Begin to write your thoughts in your journal.
7. If your thoughts are positive, write them with flourish. Feel free to doodle hearts around your message, or any kind of embellishment that feels good.
8. If you have any negative thoughts, the important thing is to finish writing each, then in large letters right after it, write the opposite of that message 3 times. For instance, if your thought was "I am lazy", your next written entry might be "I AM MOTIVATED AND AMBITIOUS!" If your thought was "I am worthless", then your next entry can be any version of "I AM WORTHY", I AM FILLED WITH SELF-WORTH", or "I AM WORTHY OF LOVE". Then draw a line through the center of the negative thought you wrote down.
9. Take a moment and write three examples underneath each negative statement that proves that statement false. For example, if I wrote, "I am lazy", I might say, "I helped a friend reorganize her basement."

Or, "I finished a work project ahead of the deadline." Or, "I wanted to lay on the couch last night and do nothing but instead, I read a book/baked cookies/did laundry/you name it." We are our own worst critics but when we take the time to acknowledge our efforts, it reminds us that we're doing the best we can.

10. Feel free to repeat this ritual while holding each crystal, or each time you come back to this ritual, engage a different crystal.

NOTES

GODDESS BATH

The point of this bath is to empower yourself and return to your inner Goddess. It will deliver strength, passion, compassion, and beauty to reconnect with your true feminine energy and sensuality. Everything you see here is what I use but feel free to eliminate what you don't have or add something that feels right to you.

What You'll Need

- Rose quartz crystal. A bunch is nice, but one will do. Promotes love, self-love, and healing.

- Carnelian crystal. A bunch is nice, but one will do. Promotes energy, passion, sensuality, and power.

- Bath salts with Bergamot, Lavender, Rose, or Ylang Ylang essential oil or a blend. If you can get your hands on some Damiana herb, put a handful in a net bag and add them to your bath (use the net so they don't cause an issue with your drain). Damiana is a strong herb that promotes sexual healing, passion, and reconnecting to your feminine power.

- Candle. Any scented candle that you love will do but the same scents as above are even better. This promotes the burning off of the old you and ushering in the new you.

- Rose petals or flower petals of any kind A bunch is nice, a handful will do. This promotes love of the self, encourages romance (Yes! By falling in love with yourself!), and infuses nature into your bathwater.

- Smudge stick for clearing your space.

- Extra towels. Place them around the bathtub to absorb spilled or splashed water.

Ritual Steps

1. Fill your bathtub with water while you set your crystals all around the rim, or you can set them around the bottom of your tub. Inside the bath water works too, =but make sure they are crystals that won't be damaged by the water (if you've purchased the accompanying Little Box of Self Love, the included crystals are water-safe).
2. Place the extra towels on the floor around the bottom of the tub.
3. Pour the salts into the bath and allow them to dissolve.
4. Add the petals to the bath (if using) and anything else you've decided to incorporate into the water.
5. Light the candle.
6. Smudge the entire area of your bath, as well as your own body.
7. Get into the bath and lay back. Breathe on a three-count in and a three-count out. At the same time, imagine your connection to the Divine, and ask for wisdom, guidance, truth, and clarity.
8. Begin noticing any thoughts that arise. If they are negative, turn them around and make them positive, or forgive yourself for whatever you think you did or should've done, or just for having the thought itself. Thank that thought and tell it that it is now

released. Sometimes when I am in a ritual, an old memory will pop up that reminds me of something I'd love to forget. I then say out loud to myself, "I forgive you and I release you." Forgiveness is important for a true release, whether for myself or someone else. Stay in this exercise for as long as it feels good.

9. After you have allowed your thoughts to arise, begin to imagine your connection to the Divine Feminine. Feel your power, sensuality, and feminine power rise to the top of the bathtub water and swirl all around you. Feel it swirl around, in, and through you.

10. Once you feel the time is right, place both hands on each side of the bathtub and forcefully stand up with all of your power but, of course, do this carefully. Yes, this will likely splash water outside the bathtub, but that's why you have those extra towels. As you rise with all of your power, allow yourself to feel your strength, balance, energy, and sovereignty while all the self-doubt, insecurities, and self-limiting thoughts stay behind in the bathwater and roll right off your skin because it no longer belongs to you.

11. Step out of the bathtub and gather anything from the bathwater you don't want going down the drain and dispose of it in the trash. While drying off, watch as the water drains from the bathtub, taking all of that which blocked your way down with the water. As it disappears, so does your fear, uncertainty, and lack of confidence. #byebye

NOTES

RELEASING RITUAL

This is an excellent ritual for ridding yourself of anything negative in your life. Whether it's another person's energy, work or personal issue, or even negative energy coming from you, this ritual will help dispel it and replenish you with love, protection, and good vibes.

What You'll Need

- Smudge stick for clearing your space

- Fireproof container

- Paper and pen

- Candle

- Small bowl of sea salt

- Small bowl of water

Ritual Steps

1. Find a time you are least likely to be interrupted and a quiet place that is comfortable for you. Smudge your space for clearing.

2. Match each object you've collected for this ritual with the element it is associated with, which then connects to a specific direction. Use a free phone compass app to identify the directions (north, east, south, west). Place the candle facing south (fire). Place the fireproof container facing east (air). The container of water should be facing west (water), and finally, the container of salt should be facing north (earth).

3. Sit in the center of your objects facing east and get still and grounded. You can do this by meditating for a few minutes or engaging in breathwork. Sit, focus, breathe, and think about whatever it is that you are ready to release.

4. Write on the paper whatever it is you would like to release. You can designate one sheet of paper per release or write it all down on one sheet. The choice is yours. While you're writing, imagine what life will be like when each of these blocks is gone. Concentrate on the feeling of releasing each burden from your life.

5. Face south and light your paper(s) with fire. Allow them to burn long enough that most of the paper is gone but not so long that you burn yourself. Place it in the fireproof container to complete its disintegration. As you watch it burn, imagine all the power these things had over you being released. Watch all of the negativity float away with the smoke.

6. Face north and pour the ash into the salt container. The salt will absorb and neutralize any leftover negative energy.

7. Turn to the west and pour the salt/ash mixture into the water for the final neutralization, and then dispose of the water mixture somewhere far from you. You can do this outside on land or flush it down the toilet. This act permanently carries these blocks away from you and out of your life.

8. Sit for a few minutes and visualize white light coming into your body through your head and down to your feet. Remember to think

or say "thank you" in gratitude for the elements taking away what no longer serves you.

9. Optionally, you can carry a Black Onyx, Black Tourmaline, Aasalt Rock, or Black Obsidian stone for protection for the next 48 hours. These crystals will absorb residue negative energy and keep it from you while grounding you.

NOTES

GRATITUDE RITUALS

Truth be told, there isn't one thing that is more powerful than gratitude. Gratitude will change your mood instantly, manifest your greatest desires, bring your biggest dreams to life, and surround you with so much joy and contentment as you've never known.

I have had conversations with some of the poorest folks I've ever met who have had more abundance than some of the wealthiest folks I know. I don't know about you, but I'll take a meaningful life filled with connection, community, love, time, laughs, memories, and loved ones over anything else.

All of this is free, and so is gratitude.

So why, if gratitude is so important is it not at the beginning of this book? Because I want this to be the last thing you walk away with. I want you to understand that any journey worth walking always begins with gratitude. Each morning or night, say a prayer of gratitude, write in a gratitude journal, murmur or whisper a "thank you" each time you think about it (I did this so much I am now in the habit of doing this all day long). However you want to send a word of Thanks out into the universe, do it. I promise you, those moments are filled with a potent magic you would never believe.

If you want to change how you feel about yourself, gratitude is a wonderful place to start.

My daughter asked me one day if I thought I was pretty. She was seven years old, and I was in a dark place on my journey. I knew I had to be very careful about what I said to her because, at that moment, she was forming everlasting impressions about what "beauty" would mean to her.. As I considered what I wanted to say, I had such a sensation of love come over me.

"Well, I definitely have good days and poopy days."

She giggled and asked, "Do you like your face, Mommy? Do you like your body?"

I answered, "Baby Love, this flabby belly grew you and brought you to life. These saggy arms rocked you to sleep every night when you were a baby. These legs filled with cellulite ran after you when you fell and hurt yourself. My body has carried me through all my years of life and seen me through all my thick and thin. I don't just *like* my body, I am in *love* with my body."

It was then that I realized how awful I had been to my beautiful, strong, amazing self. I had been mean to her; blaming her for not fitting into what culture had deemed worthy of love and happiness. Every time I walked by a mirror and winced, every nasty comment I said to myself, all the horrible thoughts and names I called myself came flooding back and I was so sad at the lifelong destructive habit I saw before me. I cried. My body cried for me and I for my body. I cried for all the things I had been mistakingly asking everyone to give to me that I wasn't willing to give to myself.

LOVE NOTES

Not long after this revelation, I began writing love notes to myself. On my worst days, I read through them and would always walk away feeling a renewed sense of love for myself.

This is your first Gratitude Ritual.

What You'll Need

- Notebook or journal

- Pen

- Smudge stick

- Rhodonite or rose quartz crystal

- Love Notes (from the Little Box of Self-Love). Optional)

Ritual Steps

1. Find a quiet place where you won't be interrupted and smudge the area and your body for clearing.
2. Sit down, and get comfortable. Read your Love Notes, if incorporating, and allow them to integrate.
3. Take a moment to reflect, then write a love note to yourself. It doesn't have to be long but it does have to be true. Some days it

might just be your eye color that you find pleasing. Other days, it might be pride for standing up and demanding to be treated with respect. Whatever it is that you write, you will find eventually that you'll have more and more and more to say. This is because you are now focusing on the *good* within yourself. Better go get a few more notebooks. ;-)

MIRROR LOVE

Mirror love is a beautiful practice in self-acknowledgment. There is a sweet simplicity in giving yourself the compliments and recognition you likely give to other women without blinking. Don't mistake its simplicity for its value; this ritual may seem easy but its effects are potent.

What You'll Need

- A mirror

- Yourself

Ritual Steps

1. Every time you walk past a mirror, stop, smile, and say something nice to yourself.

GRATITUDE RITUAL

As I mentioned previously, gratitude is the most effective practice one can have to change their perspective on oneself, their situation, or environment. When you give genuine thanks for the blessings in your life, it will shift your vibration instantly. The magic is in your authenticity.

What You'll Need

- Notebook or journal

- Pen

- Smudge stick

- Rose quartz, amethyst, and smokey quartz crystals

- Incense and incense holder, or a diffuser with Bergamot, Rose, Juniper, Ylang Ylang, Frankincense, or Lavender essential oil

Ritual Steps

1. Find a quiet place where you won't be interrupted and smudge the area and your body to clear.
2. Sit down and get comfortable. Read your Love Notes, if incorporating, and allow them to integrate.
3. Take a moment to reflect, then write what you are thankful for. This can be full sentences or a list. It can be long or short. Whatever is on

your list, be sure to notice the smile on your face that begins to form and the warmth in your heart. That's how you know it's working every time.

NOTES

Throughout this journal, you've focused on self-compassion, love, and kindness. Allow what you have learned to integrate and become a daily part of your life and continue the journey with a renewed sense of self.

Remember, this journey may never end, but with a little bit of time, focus, and practice, it can be the most rewarding experience you'll ever have.